MW00955362

Kingdom Of God and His Economy Devotional

Table of Contents

Introduction

Praise be the name of Our Father in heaven and earth! All works in power comes from Him. Our life instructions flow through the Holy Spirit dwelling within as we become portals of His words. The Kingdom family of God assemble to eat of His words so that each one will gain revelation knowledge needed for spiritual growth as one. The class of International Kingdom Mandate Ambassadors and I

Know My Assignment (IKMA) Mentorship 2022 came together in learning of His Kingdom Economy and this book is birth as contribution to His Kingdom resources. Let us be blessed of this work by meditating and capturing His divine message for each one of us. I am proud of and thank everyone who have been part of this program for His Glory!

Nancy Bocalan
IKMA USA/Philippines

A Message

It is a great opportunity to be a part of this masterpiece of Dr. Nancy Bocalan, "The Kingdom of God and His Economy" And I commend this work of art because The Kingdom of God is the answer to every need and problem of our world as King Jesus said in Matthew 6:33 But seek first the kingdom of God and His righteousness, and all these things shall be added to you. (NKJV)

And what is a Kingdom? According to Dr. Myles Munroe, "*A Kingdom is the governing influence of a king* over a territory, impacting that territory with his will, purpose, and intent, producing a culture and moral standard for his citizens."

In other words, King Jesus wants that the citizens of heaven will manifest the culture and moral standards of heaven here on earth.

The Kingdom of God is the principal subject that Jesus taught during His threeand-a-half earthly ministries. Try to read and study His parables and you can see that it's all about the Kingdom. And so, therefore, we can conclude that the Kingdom of God is the only message Jesus taught while He was still here on earth.

Luke 4:43 says, but He said to them, "I must preach the kingdom of God to the other cities also because for this purpose I have been sent" (NKJV).

Acts 1:2-3, until the day he (Jesus) was taken up to heaven, after giving instructions through the Holy Spirit to the apostles he had chosen. 3 After his suffering, he presented himself to them and gave many convincing proofs that he was alive. *He appeared to them over a period of forty days and spoke about the kingdom of God.*

In Matthew 10:7 Jesus commanded His disciples saying, "As you go, proclaim this message: 'The kingdom of heaven has come near'" (NIV).

Notice the words "this message." Jesus specified that the only message that we are to proclaim is the good news of the Kingdom.

In Matthew 24:14, King Jesus said that this gospel of the kingdom will be preached in the whole world as a testimony to all nations, and then the end will come.

The phrase the Kingdom of God tells us who owns the kingdom and obviously, it's God. God owns it. It is His will, purpose, and intention that must be done in His kingdom.

If you do not understand the concept of the Kingdom and how it works, chances are, you will be like the servant in Luke 19 who received a *mina* that instead of becoming a good steward, multiplying what his master entrusted to him, he does nothing but kept the mina and laid away in a piece of cloth (V.20).

This servant had the mindset of a slave. Instead of seeing that his master is good and generous (Vv. 17-19), he saw his master as a hard man who takes out what he did not put in and reaps what he did not sow." (V. 21).

This servant does not understand the concept of the Kingdom, that he was serving a king. And that the king is lord, the one who owns everything in his kingdom that was why he can take what he did not put in and reap what he did not sow. And the consequence of his disobedience to the king was losing what he has (V. 24).

Disagreement with the king is putting your life at risk. You may not like what the king says, but you must obey if you want to stay around and be blessed.

The Economy, on the other hand, is one of the components of the Kingdom. Just like other countries, the kingdom of God has also an economy. And the economy of the kingdom is faith. It is the currency in the Kingdom of God.

And we participate in God's economy by giving to His work and adding value to people. Thank you and more kingdom favor to all of you.

Mentor Dr. Harnold Tolentino Peñacerrada, IKMA Provincial Area Director of Iloilo City, Pastor of Kingdom Living International Ministries Iloilo, Philippines.

47 Day Devotional Words

_____

Name

NO OTHER GODS

²am the LORD thy God, which have brought thee out of the land of Egypt, out of the house of bondage. ³Thou shalt have no other gods before me.

Exodus 20:2-3

It is the Lord who delivers us from the House of Bondage, as Egypt symbolizes of a person's toiling that leads to a chaotic life. It is a dwelling place where you work in a wrong place at the wrong time. Though it is a place where you could get your bread and butter, it still it leads you to a miserable life.

I remember when I was still working as a staff on my previous job. I usually get monetary benefits and get to enjoy it with my family. But I got them by making fake documents to support the reimbursement of our funds. You see, the money I received may be an additional income in our home, but still, it came from a compromise. And this is a condition wherein; I was working at the mercy of a false god.

When we understand that there should never be another god in our lives, we then understand how important it is to be living and working in a state where God is the only Lord that we have. Because working under the leadership of God, not only gave us freedom, but He also leads us to a good and satisfying life. And most especially, to our promised land.

Prayer:

Father God, I thank you for taking me out from the bondages of this world. We thank you Father, that you have brought me back to light for me to see that in You, there I will find and experience unspeakable joy and genuine peace like no other. You truly satisfy my every need, as you guide me and walk with me back to our promised land.

In Jesus' Name, Amen.

Think of This:

God has already freed us from serving the gods of this world, we should never return in serving them in whatever thing we do.

FORSAKE FOR HIS' SAKE

28And Jesus said unto them, Verily I say unto you, That ye which have followed me, in the regeneration when the Son of man shall sit in the throne of his glory, ye also shall sit upon twelve thrones, judging the twelve tribes of Israel. 29And everyone that hath forsaken houses, or brethren, or sisters, or father, or mother, or wife, or children, or lands, for my name's sake, shall receive a hundredfold, and shall inherit everlasting life. Matthew 19:28-29

The greatest challenge in the Kingdom of God is to submit and follow the King. As abundant life in the Kingdom of God requires not just your faith and allegiance to the King, but also a total surrender of your will, properties and all that is about you.

We often look at the promises found in the scripture, but we seldom look at the requirements needed from us to have it.

Just like the young man who's asking Jesus on how to have an everlasting life. Most of the time, what we think of giving is what we can do, or what can we get done with our abilities and talents. But what God is asking from us is everything about us.

To receive a hundred-fold, it requires your everything. For the Kingdom of God will cause to radically change your condition in life as you go extreme in obeying the King's required submission. And in the above passage, a total submission of your whole being and what you have is the key to experiencing the extraordinary, exceedingly, abundant life that can only be found in the Kingdom of God.

Prayer:

Father, our King, thank you for reminding me that without You, I am nothing. And that all that I have and possess all came from You, therefore, they belong to You. Today, I surrender everything about me in Your hands. And I thank You, Lord, that You allowed me to be the steward of these things that I have here with me.

In Jesus' Name, Amen.

Think of This:

We are only stewards of the things we have now, because the One who owns everything is God alone.

GIVE AND BE GIVEN

³⁸Give, and it shall be given unto you; good measure, pressed down, and shaken together, and running over, shall men give into your bosom. For with the same measure that ye mete withal it shall be measured to you again. Luke 6:38

Money talks has become a sensitive issue inside every ministry or church. Many has become afraid that leaders who teach about giving gives them the feeling as if they are being fraud to give.

But giving is a communal responsibility, especially as a citizen in the Kingdom of God. It is like a barter change, design to meet a need in a community. Your participation in giving qualifies you to receive something in return. It is when we buy, we pay the cost, or we give the amount of value of the thing that we want to purchase.

And a healthy exchange or trading, as we call it now, helps us grow, develop, and empower the economy of the community we live in.

If we try to understand it deeply, giving is a good system that keeps the Kingdom economy circulating in good measure. It is a beautiful key that benefits not just the giver but those who also belong to the community, as it may result to a great influence that could inspire others to follow suit, as this will lead to an economic abundance that shall benefit the whole community.

Prayer:

Lord, thank you for helping me understand that giving is not a burden that was being passed on to me, but a pass for me to take part in the growth of Your Kingdom Economy.

In Jesus Christ's Name, Amen

Think of This:

Everybody in a community, whether rich or poor, take part in their trading system so they can sustain their needs in their homes. The Kingdom of God is no different, as it also has a government and a community.

THE HIGHER POWER

¹Let every soul be subject unto the higher powers. For there is no power but of God: the powers that be are ordained of God. Romans 13:1

It is important to submit on physical governmental authorities for such power was allowed by God. It is somewhat an opportunity for us to practice our obedience because if we find it hard to submit on a physical government, how much more can we obey to a spiritual government which is unseen.

There may be some who does not follow simple road signs, or basic posted warnings, but that should never be an excuse for you to disobey as well. Remember, even not knowing a certain law, will not excuse a person from following it.

However, there may come a time, that even this government we reside in, truly can fail us. Corrupted officials, Unreasonable price hikes, crimes, and injustices. Things like these will challenge our faith in our physical government.

But since God is the King of justice, He will not forsake you but will always watch over you. The King Himself shall be your weighing scale, so whenever our physical government fails us, He will be there to save you and tend to your needs. God, the King shall take responsibility over you, for He is the one who allowed such authority to be manifested on Earth. So be still and know that He is God!

Prayer:

Father, I thank you for this assurance that in this corrupted and unjust world, I can still trust that You will never leave me nor forsake me. I thank you, Father, for knowing that You are always on my side, as I live in this world.

In Jesus' Name, Amen

Think of This:

You belong in the Kingdom of Heaven, making you a citizen of Heaven. So, remember that God is looking after you.

SUPPLIED RICHES

19But my God shall supply all your need according to his riches in glory by Christ Jesus.
Philippians 4:19

There will come a point in our lives as if, there is no help, you feel hopeless, especially when you feel like, you are lacking in your finances.

These times will make you feel stuck in a situation that, it is as if, you can do nothing, and you cannot go on, even just to pursue God's calling for you.

But our God is King and Lord over all. And this is the reason why He can, and He is able to supply whatever needs we have. He is the Creator, meaning, He owns all of Creation. He owns the silver, the gold, and all things on earth, He is the LORD Most High, and at His command, the Earth shakes.

This is how wonderful our God is. Though, sometimes, difficulties in our lives tend to cover up this truth. But hey, God is the Hope of all hearts. The LORDSHIP of Christ secures us from famine and crisis. Since, He is the owner of all that is in Earth, He is more than capable of supplying all our needs. So always remember, God got you!

Prayer:

Lord of all the Earth, thank you God for securing that you can give whatever we are lacking, if just we believe. Thank you, Lord, that for this reason, I will always trust in You.

In Jesus' Name, Amen.

Think of This:

Isn't it great to have a Father that owns everything? And because of that, we will lack nothing.

CAESAR'S and GOD'S

[17]And Jesus answering said unto them, Render to Caesar the things that are Caesar's, and to God the things that are God's. And they marveled at him. Mark 12:17

As we are living in the physical world, under a physical government, we are of course, subjected to all the laws and obligations as part of being its citizen. That includes paying our dues and taxes. So, if we can give what this government requires of us, much more that God is more worthy to receive from us, isn't it?

As we read the passage above, it states that the people should give to Caesar what are his, and to God what are God's. And, meaning also. Therefore, if we submit to our nation's policies, then we too, are to give to our King, because we also call ourselves citizens of His Kingdom.

Whatever we enjoy today, all the things that we have, even our breath, they all came from God. He is the rightful owner of everything, and we are just His stewards.

This is the reason why it is necessary for us to understand God's Lordship. How we recognize that nothing really belongs to us will also be beneficial for us. Because it will be easy to submit to the Lordship System of God. For because of His Lordship, the Kingdom of God becomes invincible.

Prayer:

Dear Lord, thank you for reminding me that I should never neglect my obligation as part of your Kingdom. Thank you for providing for me your citizen and thank you for reminding me that I am part of how Your Kingdom is unshakable.

Think of This:

If every citizen participates and do their part in the Kingdom of God, then God as King will make sure that every need and the welfare of His citizens are met.

TO THE STOREHOUSE

10Bring ye all the tithes into the storehouse, that there may be meat in mine house, and prove me now herewith, saith the LORD of hosts, if I will not open you the windows of heaven, and pour you out a blessing, that there shall not be room enough to receive it. Malachi 3:10

Tithing, however sensitive this topic may be, is crucial in the Kingdom of God, for it enables man to show his loyalty and obedience to the King. It also allows the Kingdom of God to continually operate in a man's life.

In any country, a livelihood or a business is required to have permits and declare their taxes so that, their company will have the right to operate, and have security as well from the government against fraud and other criminal offenses committed to them.

This goes the same with the Kingdom of God. The reason why we say that tithes or tithing is a tither's security, is because, God, the King, has set His laws against all greedy, covetous and thief, and He will make sure that justice will always be served.

Tithing also results to breakthrough and abundance in one's welfare. And this welfare helps a man to develop progressively as a good citizen of the Kingdom of God. Tithing benefits the whole community because its goal is to have a commonwealth within the community.

Prayer:

Lord, my King, thank you for letting me understand that tithing is necessary in your Kingdom. That it will not only support any ministry but will benefit our community. Not only for my welfare and security, but also for the abundance and growth of my brethren's progress.

Think of This:

A community under a commonwealth of a King will not only satisfy our needs but will help us look out for one another.

CHEERFUL GIVER

*⁷Every man according as he purposeth in his heart, so let him give;
not grudgingly, or of necessity: for God loveth a cheerful giver. 2
Corinthians 9:7*

The receiver can always tell if the one who gives has happily given away or is just giving out of necessity. And a cheerful giver is the one that God will always acknowledge for it brings joy to Him.

This is the reason why tithing is different from an offering. The tithes are for the government, making it a necessity or an obligation for the citizens to pay, or return. However, offering is what we give to the King. And offering does not always talk about money.

The King does not look at the amount you give, but in the attitude of the heart of the giver. He doesn't look at how great you are, He is looking at how willing you are to spend it on Him, your talents, time, and treasures.

If we don't want to waste our offering to God, then, we must have a heart that is always cheerful for this makes our offering good and pleasing to the King.

Prayer:

God, thank you for letting me know that telling how much You are worth to me will be more special if I am to give you something out of the abundance of my heart. That whatever my heart happily offers to You will not go to waste but will be pleasing and treasured by You.

In Jesus' Name, Amen.

Think of This:

We bring joy to God if we are full of joy when we are giving to Him.

SEEK FIRST

33But seek ye first the kingdom of God, and his righteousness; and all these things shall be added unto you. Matthew 6:33

No obedient follower of the law or even a government has become wealthy. There is no citizen in any government, that has been granted wealth, just because of his submission to the law.

But, in the Kingdom of God, the importance of seeking His Kingdom first, lies on you, trying to see, know, and understand what is in God's mind. What is it that's running in the mind of my King? What plan could it be that my Father, has designed for me? Then that will help you position yourself rightfully in your supposed path. At that point, everything will follow and be provided for you.

We oftentimes, focus on every promise that was written in the Bible. We always try to look for things on how we will be able to overcome life difficulties, and we end up not understanding that God requires something from us first. God does not plan for His citizens to face hardships, but not knowing God's plan for you will lead you nowhere.

So, seek His Kingdom now, position yourself in your right standing, and you will experience ease.

Prayer:

Father, thank you for letting me know that the reason why I face hardships in life is because I am going against of Your original plan for me. Thank you for making me understand that in Your Kingdom, there will I find the truth, and Your purpose for me.

In Jesus' Name, Amen.

Think of This: seek His Kingdom, position yourself, and you experience ease.

LOVING GOD

⁴Hear, O Israel: The LORD our God, the LORD is one.
⁵Love the LORD your God with all your heart and with all your soul and with all your strength.
⁶These commandments that I give you today are to be on your hearts.
Deuteronomy 6:4-6

The reason why Jesus said that it will be hard for the rich man to enter the kingdom of God was because, when you allow your wealth to be god, and you tend to rely on your own self sufficiency, then what else can God do for you?

Understanding that God, is King, and Lord overall, and knowing that He too is your Father, will make us dependent on Him solely. And that is what He wants from us to do to Him. He, being One and all, is the only One that we need in our lives.

God wants us to understand that being the owner of everything, wants His sons to be the stewards of His property. And for this, we must do our part to be involve using the potential He has invested in us.

God is showing us His love by sharing to us what He owns, and our part is to also show our love for Him, in the same manner. Everything about us, all that we are, all that we have, all that we have accomplished is His.

Prayer:

Father God, thank you for this expression of Your great love to me. Thank you, Father, for setting an example, so that we may know Your heart.

In Jesus' Name, Amen.

Think of This:

God first loved us so that we can express His love not only on what we do, but to others as well.

The Prayer

This, then, is how you should pray; Our Father in heaven hollowed be your name.
-MATTHEW 6:9

This is a prayer of a Son to his Father who is in heaven. Jesus wants us to remember every time we pray that we have a heavenly Father who loves us unconditionally. We share our heavenly Father with other believe. We have brothers and sisters in the spiritual family God has given us, through them we find strength and encouragement we need to face the ups and downs of our journey here on earth. God has called us to love and care our kingdom family in the same way Jesus loved us.

A new command I give you; Love one another. As I have loved you, so you must love one another.
-JOHN 13:34

We must pray to our Father with concern to our brothers and sisters here on earth.

He also wants them to enjoy His Kingdom like we do. He wants His children to enjoy the abundant life He has prepared for us; He only wants what is best for us.

Prayer:

Thank you, Jesus, for teaching us how to pray to our Father in heaven, help us also pray for our brothers and sisters especially those who are not yet in your Kingdom so they can enjoy your Love. Amen!

Think of This:

He told us to pray always and, we must pray for our families (brothers and sisters) because we are all his children, that He loves unconditionally and as a loving Father He can provide everything we need in this world and unto eternity with Him.

The Father's Will

Your Kingdom come, your will be done, on earth as it is in heaven.
-MATTHEW 6:10

The Father has a Kingdom in heaven that He rules. He is a God of love. He wants to be in that Kingdom, to experience Him as Love. This is a prime reason why he created earth and made man so that earth shall be just like heaven.

He created us in His image and likeness to dominate or rule earth for His will to be done here on earth through us; His children as it is in heaven. His will is for man to return to Him, regain understanding of their identity, enjoy their inheritance which is the Kingdom of God and walk with restored dominion mandate. In His Kingdom we are to make God the Lord (owner, source) of our lives. Let us make Him the Lord of our life, pray for His complete rule over our families, our neighbor, our classmates, and our friends until everyone shall acknowledge Him as our Lord.

When we pray this prayer, we as Kingdom citizens, must be prepared to be answers and solutions as God's kingdom extension here on earth. We shall be living as Christ ambassadors working to expand Hs kingdom wherever we go.

Prayer:

Thank you, Father, that your Kingdom is now here inside us because, the Holy Spirit is now residing inside of us. We are are your temples and Your Kingdom is now manifesting and invading the earth through us. Amen!

Think of This:

We are not only to pray but we must go and share that the Kingdom of God is at hand and is within us.

Our Daily Bread

Give us today our daily bread.
-MATTHEW 6:11

Bread is the common served food for many people, but here in our country Philippine's rice is our staple food and we have it every day and usually not just once a day but every meal. As His disciples follow Him daily, they ate of the natural bread but also received their daily food represented by the demonstration of His works and power with revelation pertaining to life in the Kingdom.

They had seen Jesus heal diseases, calm the storm, raise the dead, walk on water and a lot more. But Jesus was telling them and us that we must not leave God out of the seemingly ordinary parts of life. It pleases God to hear us praying every day for our daily bread.

It is a way that we rely on God for everything, not just the big things but the everyday needs in life. We acknowledge Him as our source, or supplier and owner of all things.

Our Father loves us, and He wants to take care of our needs and even our wants, whether we need a miracle or supernatural things or a piece of bread. Remember that everything in life is from Him.

Prayer:

Thank you, Father, for being our source of everything in this life, thank you for always providing not only big things but every detail of our lives. You are our source and supplier. Amen!

Think of This:

Don't forget to thank Him today and each day for meeting our needs in all aspects of our lives, spiritual, physical, emotional, intellectual, and financial material.

Forgiveness

Forgive us our debts, as we also have forgiven our debtors.
-MATTHEW 6:12

The world has lots of phrases to describe our reactions when someone hurts us or mistreats us. For example: "I'll get you for that!", "One day you will get yours!" Or "Don't get mad, get even!" But Jesus shows us a better way. It is called forgiveness, He calls on us to forgive those who offended us, just as God has forgiven us as He continues to forgive our sins against Him.

God promises us that we will be treated the same way we treat others. (MATTHEW 7:2; LUKE 6:37-38) If we are generous towards others, we will experience God's generosity. If we refuse to forgive those who wronged us, God will not forgive our sins, because he loves and wants us to develop our character matching His (because we are created in His image and likeness). God is perfectly just that He won't treat us one way and yet allow us to treat others in a different way. The Sonship prayer reminds us that if we hope to receive forgiveness, we must be willing to extend forgiveness as well.

If you are holding on to bitterness, refusing to forgive someone, look within your heart how God overlooked your sin when He made you, His Child.

Prayer:

Thank you, Father, for giving us the command of forgiveness that when we obey, we will experience the freedom and the joy of forgiving those who hurt us. We are free to enjoy your blessings when we forgive. Amen.

Think of This:

Now He is asking you to do the same and pardon the sin of your debtor, and when you let go of a grudge, you will experience the joy and freedom that comes with forgiveness.

Divine Protection from Temptation

And lead us not into temptation but deliver us from evil one. -
MATTHEW 6:13

Temptation is everywhere and a time will come or may have come already when you find yourself facing intense temptation. You may be asked to compromise in sex, lying, stealing, or gossiping. Others may pressure you to get into alcohol, drugs, or gambling, in our generation today many people also drink alcohol met like before, you may not have been looking for it, but suddenly the powerful voice of temptation is calling out to you and see that you are on the edge of giving in. Also, through peer-pressure if your friends are doing these things, you feel that you need to do it also. God knows about the temptations we will face; he sees all about what we are doing.

God looks down from heaven on the sons of men to see if there are any who understand, any who seek God. –PSALMS 53:2

Knowing the danger of encountering temptations, He will direct us across or away from it to keep us safe. However, we must pursue to avoid temptation and evil. The enemy and darkness is after our destruction. At times of temptations, we think we will be strong enough to pull back at the last minute yet find out that we are trapped into it. When we walk towards our destiny, we realize that temptation is not easily resisted as we thought. It can be a much more powerful foe than we realize during it. We must daily ask God to keep us from situations that can overpower us and to make us stronger to conquer it through Him.

Prayer:
Thank you, Lord, for keeping us safe and guiding us to the right path and delivering us from evil one. We trust you with our whole life because we know you love us. Amen!

Think of This:
Ask Him to guide you into his will and away from all that distract or destroy us. David prayed with sincerity in (PSALMS 25, 23 AND 27).

The Vine

I am the vine; you are the branches. If a man remains in me and I in him, he will bear much fruit; apart from me you can do nothing.
-JOHN 15:5

God wants His children to remain in Him; to grow or mature in their personal relationship with Him and spread the word of the Kingdom of God here on earth. We tend to do these things in our own strength. We are so busy trying to do things for God that we have no time to spread the word of God. Jesus' message is straightforward just as an electric tool is useless without electricity, so the Christian life is impossible without the presence and guidance of Christ trough the Holy Spirit in us. Jesus says "Abide in me" it can't be done alone. Jesus says we need to take a lesson from a branch, when a branch is receiving everything, the vine must give, the fruit come naturally and effortlessly.

The key to the Christian life is not as hard when we try to be spiritual but how closely we stay connected to Christ. We need not worry so much about what we are doing. Focus should be on staying close to Christ. When we enjoy a close relationship with Christ, He can produce all kinds of good things in our lives. Focus on strengthening our relationship with the vine and the fruit will be come forth naturally.

Prayer:

Thank you, Lord, for this verse that we can be effective in this life if we are connected to you. Help us to remain connected to you so we can bear much fruit. Amen!

Think of This:

Remember, apart from the vine, the branch is only a declaration.

Glorifying the Father

This is to my Father's glory, that you bear much
fruit, showing yourselves to be my disciples. -JOHN
15:8

You may be a brand-new Christian, or you've known Jesus for years already. Being a true citizen of the Kingdom of God should become obvious to others that you belong to Jesus. When people look at you, they should see evidence that God is at work in your life. What kind of evidence? Jesus called it fruit. Because the Holy Spirit is now residing inside of you, the fruit of the Holy Spirit will normally be seen in your life. When you put others first instead of yourself, that is fruit. When you get rid of an ungodly habit and seek to live a pure/holy life, that's fruit. When you forgive others who hurt you instead of cursing, that's fruit. When you refuse gossip but choose to build up others, that's fruit. When you control your temper, even when others lose theirs, that's fruit. The types of fruits in The Spirit are endless.

God doesn't expect you to produce all the fruit on your own. Jesus said you're not capable apart from Him living a life that glorifies the Father. We must cooperate to the leading of the Holy Spirit in your life to see amazing things happen. But if we resist to His leading, we will not produce fruit in our lives.

Prayer:
Thank you, Lord for the Holy Spirit, in me that I can now produce fruit that remain and fruit that glorifies your Name. Amen!

Think of This:
Are you the same person then or have you allowed God to produce fruit in your life as a testimony of His generation?

Chosen to Bear Fruit

You did not choose me, but I chose you and appointed you to go and bear fruit- fruit that will last. Then the Father will give you whatever you ask in my name.
-JOHN 15:16

Do you remember the thrill of knowing that out of all who could have been selected, you were the one preferred to receive the honor? If you are a Christian, you are selected to receive the highest honor and blessing possible, you are a child of the King. God chose you out of all the millions of people who populated the earth- past, present, and future. God noticed you and determined that should be His.

Now you are His, bought with a price and very valuable to Him. As God's chosen child you have a new purpose to make a difference in His Kingdom. You are to go bear fruit and share the gospel of the Kingdom of God. We are chosen to go and continue to undergo discipleship training, a process to make us more like Christ and have an intimate relationship to our Father.

He wants your life to be like Christ life, a transformed life from the inside and out, living a life that brings glory to our Father in all aspect of our lives, in thoughts, in words and in deeds. He expects us to have disciples like us, having the same transformed life imparted to the next generation- these are the fruits that we pass on for the next generation.

Prayer:
Thank you, Lord, for choosing me and command me to go and bear fruit, help me to do my assignment and make more disciples like me in your Kingdom. Amen!

Think of This:
The Kingdom life is the abundant life that Jesus promised to us.

Divine Provision

And my God will meet all your needs according to his glorious riches in Christ
Jesus.
-PHILIPPIANS 4:19

Paul was writing a thank you note to his good friend in Philippians, they'd
taken up a collection to help Him continue serving as a missionary in another
city. As he commands them that God would in turn, be generous with them.

As the apostle Paul who known that the owner of everything here and in
heaven is the Lord says that His God and our God will provide all our needs
because He is a generous God. God's math is different from us and others. We
think the more we give away the less we have, God says be generous, because
the more you give, the more I will give you. You can't out give God. Giving your
tithes is just telling God you are the owner of my money. Be a giver like our
creator and enjoy His generosity in all aspect of your life, tithing is more about
fruit and heart issue. Because the bible says there are 2 masters, God, and
money. When God asks you to give away something or to share what you have,
don't worry that you'll come up short.

Prayer:

Thank you, Lord, for being so generous to me and to all your children,
helps us to be like you especially in our finances. We will give generously and
with a cheerful heart. Amen!

Think of This:

God is the owner, and you are only a steward. so he will take care of all
your needs as His storehouse never gets empty.

Living with God

The Lord was with Joseph and He prospered,
and he lived in the house of his Egyptian master.
-GENESIS 39:2

The Bible said that God was with Joseph. This is significant considering Joseph's situation. His father assumed he was dead. His brother has no idea where he was. His mother was dead. He was alone no twins; he was in prison on a false charge. Joseph discovered that even when everyone else abandoned him God remained, God made His presence with Joseph obvious through what He did in Joseph's life. Joseph did not have an easy life, but He blessed him. When Joseph was a slave, God made him chiefs' slave. When Joseph was a prisoner, he became assistant to the jailer. When there seemed little reason to have confidence God gave Joseph courage.

God's presence doesn't mean you won't experience hard times. It doesn't mean that no matter what you are going through because you know that He is with you just as Joseph knew he was not alone- God is with Him. God's presence will give you security when everything is going wrong, His love will be obvious to you even when it seems no one else cares. God's wisdom will guide you to make the right choices in the confusion of life. The bible says Joseph prospered because God was with Him, God's presence will make an obvious difference in your life as well.

Prayer
Thank you, Lord, for always being with me at all times in all seasons of my life. I'm assured and secured for your presence is always with me. Amen!

Think of This:
No matter how tough your circumstances be confident of what you can have because God is with you. Amen!

Man, the Reflection of GOD

"And God said, Let us make man in our image, after our likeness: and let them have dominion…So God created man in his own image, in the image of God created he him; male and female created he them." Genesis 1:26-27, King James Version Bible.

We are beings formed from the earth and made alive by the breath of GOD, created with the spoken purpose of our being the image of GOD. Created to be a visible reflection of and representation of GOD in the physical and spiritual realm.

We are a product of GOD's creative, companionable, compassionate nature contained in an earthly body. We are children of our FATHER GOD who loves us so much they that we are purposed to reflect the divinity of GOD our creator.

Prayer:

FATHER GOD, Thank YOU for creating me in YOUR image and likeness. Help me to reflect YOU in all my being, so others will see and know that YOU are GOD. Teach me to reproduce YOUR: Presence, Word, and Power in the community here on earth. I ask these things in Jesus' name – Amen.

Think on this:

You are the visible image, the reflection, of the invisible GOD!

Father GOD, Thank You for creating me in your image and likeness. Help me to reflect You in all my being, so others will see and know that You are GOD. Teach me to reproduce Your Divine Presence, Word, and Power in the community here on earth. I ask these things in Jesus' name – Amen!

Think of This:

List three of your characteristics that reflect the image of GOD.

1.

2.

3.

Kingdom Economy Community

"May God Almighty bless you and make you fruitful and increase your numbers until you become a community of peoples." Genesis 28:3, NIV

Economy can be explained as an asset management of differing resources and economic agencies.

GOD's economy is HIS kingdom communities which are both resources and economic agencies.

Community economy is God's creation of a family unit that shares a common identity in Christ Jesus; and is created with a shared purpose, and common objective of glorifying our Creator through reproducing, managing, and expanding HIS kingdom. Community is a living organism made up of many members and differing types of members (human, plant, animal, spiritual) yet, existing as one.

Prayer:

Lord Jesus, it is in You that all creation is unified into one community, Thank You! Lord, I want to know and understand my assignment so that I can take my rightful place in the oneness of Our FATHER's kingdom community.

Think of This:

Jesus prays "I pray that they will all be one, just as You and I are one - as you are in me, Father, and I am in You. And may they be in us so that the world will believe you sent me." - John 17:21 New Living Translation Bible

God's Economy Stewardship

Genesis 1:28, Amplified Bible Version: "And God blessed them [granting them certain authority] and said to them, "Be fruitful, multiply, and fill the earth, and subjugate it [putting it under your power]; and rule over (dominate) the fish of the sea, the birds of the air, and every living thing that moves upon the earth."

The Kingdom of GOD has laws and a governmental system that must be upheld and enforced, to perpetuate, expand and benefit the kingdom and its citizens.

Ruler and Rulership - "Give the king Your judgements. O GOD, and Your righteousness to the king's son may he judge your people with righteousness and your afflicted with justice...May he also rule from sea to sea...to the ends of the earth...he will rescue the needy when he cries for help, the afflicted and abused also...he will have compassion on the poor and he will save the lives of the needy...He will redeem their life from oppression, fraud and violence, and their blood will be precious in his sight." Psalms 72: 1- 14, King James Version Bible Man's dominion and rulership authority is not defined in the terms of ownership or control; stewardship and caretaking are better terms to help understand man's responsibility to manage GOD's earthly realm.

"'[Stewardship]…where a person looks after another's affairs (resources).' The Greek definition of economy is stewardship, administration, and household management." – Nancy B. Bocalan

Prayer:

Father GOD, help me to truly grasp the meaning of stewardship over the things that belong to You. Teach me by Your Holy Spirit to manage, reproduce and expand the resources You have entrusted to my keeping. Thank You Father, for giving me the example of Your son Jesus to follow – Amen.

Think of this:

List three ways you can exercise stewardship:

1.
2.
3.

God's Kingdom Economic System Design-Manage His Resources

The Kingdom economy is based on the principles of reproducing and multiplying. Now to help us better understand:

Kingdom Economic System – the means by which kingdom resources are managed. "It is a system that originated from the Creator, who applied Himself as its foundation by allocating and distributing His Spirit to the visible man. He also demonstrated management of order when he placed creation in its designed places and assignments...and dispersed them accordingly – 'to be fruitful and multiply...'" - Nancy B. Bocalan "Managing Earth In Heaven." Genesis 1:11, 22, 24, 28, King James Version Bible: "And God said, Let the earth bring forth grass, the herb yielding seed, and the fruit tree yielding fruit after his kind, whose seed is in itself, upon the earth: and it was so. 22 And God blessed them, saying, Be fruitful, and multiply, and fill the waters in the seas, and let fowl multiply in the earth. 24 And God said, Let the earth bring forth the living creature after his kind, cattle, and creeping thing, and beast of the earth after his kind: and it was so. 28 And God blessed them, and God said unto them, Be fruitful, and multiply, and replenish the earth, and subdue it: and have dominion over the fish of the sea, and over the fowl of the air, and over every living thing that moveth upon the earth."

Prayer:

FATHER GOD, help me to be still and wait on YOUR Holy Spirit to illuminate what YOU have placed within me. Guide me into the truth of YOUR purposes and my assignment in caring for Your creation in Jesus' name – Amen.

Think of This:

Stop here, take some time to seek understanding from The Holy Spirit; meditate and reflect on what has been shared.

Kingdom Advancement-Plant, See, Sprout, Fruit, Harvest, Repeat

"Now the promises were spoken to Abraham and to his seed. He does not say, "And to seeds," as one would in referring to many, but rather as in referring to one, "And to your seed," that is, Christ." Galatians 3:16, New American Standard Bible

"Zera" the Hebrew word for Seed used in the book of Genesis and defined as anything that [contains the potential to] produce new life (reproduction). "Reproduction the process where a new individual organism is produced by its parents." – JBYU's

Other words that can be defined as "seed" are:

"Concept" something conceived in the [Creator's] mind, plan, and intention.

"Genesis" origin or mode of formation, creation coming into being, source.

"Embryo" a stage of development after fertilization but before birth. Man like a tree yielding fruit.

Trees bearing fruit with seed in them according to their kind represents GOD'S blueprint for Kingdom   growth and development. GOD's geneses supply the tree (Christ) with His seed (Word of GOD) and germinate the seed (death, burial, resurrection); allowing time for the seedlings (disciples) to mature through all stages of development from an embryo to ripe fruit (produce); a seed-bearing structure that can be harvested (reaped) as the multiplied means of replenishing (sowing) GOD's Kingdom Community.

"And he [man] shall be like a tree firmly planted [and tended] by the streams of water, ready to bring forth its fruit in its season; its leaf also shall not fade or wither; and everything he does shall prosper [and come to maturity]." Psalm 1:3, Amplified Bible Classic Edition

Prayer:

Father GOD, teach me to be the best cultivator of YOUR Seed. I need to learn how to prepare the soil for optimal Seed growth. Lord, as I grow and mature becoming fruit, let me always acknowledge that growth and increase comes only through your provision. Please Lord, send more laborers into Your harvest. I ask all in Jesus' name. – Amen

Think on This:

Reflect on the Divine Image, Reproductive Power and Dominion of Our FATHER, and His Christ, Our King, and Tree of Life.

Assignment of The Seed-To Sprout

"11 For as the earth brings forth its sprouts, and as a garden cause what is sown in it to sprout up, so the Lord GOD will cause righteousness and praise to sprout up before all the nations." Isaiah 61:11

Breaking through uncultivated soil, a newly sprouted seedling's life is dependent on seeking sunlight nutrients and stability to grow. Babes in Christ like the sprout, hopes for the same things, warmth, nourishment, and the stability of a safe home. The new seedling is like a child that is born into the family of GOD exemplifying how we must all live in utter dependence upon the Lord, drawing our nurture and guidance from our heavenly father.

"…It takes time and patience to plant a seed and wait for the plant to rise and become full in its expression. But, as you all know, the feelings and results of this are astonishing and beautiful. Waiting and witnessing a new life form to come to life and reveal its splendor." www.rareplant.me

"Then it sprouted and became a low, spreading vine with its branches turned toward him, but its roots remained under it. So, it became a vine and yielded shoots and sent out branches." Ezekiel 17:6

Prayer:

Thank YOU FATHER, just as YOU planted Christ, He plants me in good soil and waters me with YOUR Word. Lord Jesus, Your light has drawn me from the soil and caused me to sprout up. Lord, mature me into fruit that I may nurture and protect the Seed of The Word, and reproduce for the glory of GOD'S Kingdom. – Amen

Think of This:

"Beloved, now are we the sons of God, and it doth not yet appear what we shall be: but we know that, when he shall appear, we shall be like him [Christ]…" 1 John 3:2

Devotionals by Arnna Williams Frazier   **Day 27**

Kingdom Foundation-Love

The Way of Love Discipleship

"I am the true vine, and my Father is the husbandman. [2] Every branch in me that beareth not fruit he taketh away: and every branch that beareth fruit, he purgeth it, that it may bring forth more fruit. [3] Now ye are clean through the word which I have spoken unto you. [4] Abide in me, and I in you. As the branch cannot bear fruit of itself, except it abide in the vine; no more can ye, except ye abide in me. [5] I am the vine, ye are the branches: He that abideth in me, and I in him, the same bringeth forth much fruit: for without me ye can do nothing. [6] If a man abides not in me, he is cast forth as a branch, and is withered; and men gather them, and cast them into the fire, and they are burned. [7] If ye abide in me, and my words abide in you, ye shall ask what ye will, and it shall be done unto you. [8] Herein is my Father glorified, that ye bear much fruit; so, shall ye be my disciples. [9] As the Father hath loved me, so have I loved you: continue ye in my love. [10] If ye keep my commandments, ye shall abide in my love; even as I have kept my Father's commandments and abide in his love. [11] These things have I spoken unto you, that my joy might remain in you, and that your joy might be full. [12] This is my commandment, that ye love one another, as I have loved you." John 15:1-12, King James Version
"[34] A new commandment I give unto you, that ye love one another; as I have loved you, that ye also love one another." John 13:34, King James Version:

Prayer:

FATHER GOD, teach us to love one another as you have loved us and to give the best of all we are and must secure our brothers and sisters for YOUR Kingdom. In Jesus name, Amen.

Think of This:

CHILDREN OF GOD, HIS LOVE HAS GIVEN US THE KINGDOM, TO GOD BE THE GLORY! AMEN.

Hallelujah!

I believe that God owns it all, my finances, my influence, my everything, and I will be held accountable for my faithfulness in using his resources, time, talent, treasure. Truth and relationships are gifts to be stewarded for the ultimate glory of him. Stewardship includes an additional concern, caring for something that God put impression on me, for there is nothing I/we own apart from Him. (John 12:10, 2Corinthians 4:7, 1Corinthians 6:19). God owns everything and ultimately all things belong to God that He entrusts me with resources and responsibilities to steward for His glory and that expectation to Him, to help me resolve irritations, anger, worry and fear. That, hence, He allows me to develop sense of responsibility, accountability and of course reward.

God stewardship is being mentioned in Genesis 1:28 God blessed them and said to them. "Be fruitful and increase in number; fill the earth and subpanel it. Rule fish of the sea and the birds of the air and over every living creature that moves on the ground." And that's my responsibility and mandate from God.

Giving back what is due to God is not only an expression of obedience but of gratitude, trust and increasing joy and part of my worship to God. (2 Corinthians 9:6-8 a cheerful giver with joy).

I believe God wants me to spend His money to develop and maintain my family, my kingdom family, and my well-being. (See Matthew 6:33)

Prayer:

I say yes to God above and before everything that matters in His life and so seeking God's kingdom, calls us to evangelize, seeking His righteousness and foster basic Christian act and compassion to feed the poor, both spiritual and physical. The point is that putting God's concerns ahead of my own, seeking His agenda with all my heart, because I believe and trust His provision over all the matters of my life as what He promised me. AMEN!

Think of This:

I consider myself as owner of God's blessings to me, my life, my health, material blessings, my joy; but a part of that is my responsibility to bless other people too, to share His word, my joy, and both of my material blessings I received; "it pass on practice", "you learned – you teach", "you're earned – you give."

Abundant Life

The thief does not come except to steal, and to kill, and to destroy. I have come that they may have life, and that they may have *it* more abundantly. - John 10:10 KJV

*"**More abundantly**"* means to have superabundance of a thing.

Abundant life refers to life in its abounding fullness of joy and strength for spirit, soul, and body. Abundance of God means seeking after God and its goodness, continual process of hearing, practicing, and maturing as well as failing, recovering, adjusting, enduring, and overcoming.

Now to him who can do immeasurably more than all we ask or imagine, according to his power that is at work within us, - Ephesians 3:20 NIV

Prayer:
Lord Thank you for many ways you bless us and letting us know that abundant life is the result of having been made new; that we have Christ in us. Amen!

Think of This:
God never abandon us.

Transformation and Renewing of Mind

Because of the LORD's great love, we are not consumed, for his compassions never fail. They are new every morning; great is your faithfulness. - Lamentations 3:22-23 NIV

It reminds us that God's compassion and His mercies are new every morning. Every single morning is a gift; that each day we could approach the King and say, "Your will will be done today and not mine, Lord!"

Therefore, get rid of all moral filth and the evil that is so prevalent and humbly accept the word planted in you, which can save you. -James 1:21 NIV

Prayer:

Dear Lord, Thank You that you let us begin again and again because your mercies are new every morning. Amen!

Think of This:

God gives us second chances.

Wait!

...but those who hope in the LORD will renew their strength. They will soar on wings like eagles; they will run and not grow weary; they will walk and not be faint.

- Isaiah 40:31 NIV

As we wait upon the Lord, we grow in knowledge of Him and His command for us: diligently to seek Him and apply His laws.

To hope and trust in the Lord requires faith, patience, humility, meekness, long-suffering, keeping the commandment and enduring up to the end.

To wait upon the means to plant the seed of faith and nourishing expectation.

"The King will reply, 'Truly I tell you, whatever you did for one of the least of these brothers and sisters of mine, you did for me.' -Matthew 25:40 NIV

Prayer:

Father thank you for when you ask me to wait you where there alongside of me. Amen!

Think of This:

Even in the waiting, God is working.

You have been Called Tonight

For if you remain silent at this time, relief and deliverance for the Jews will arise from another place, but you and your father's family will perish. And who knows but that you have come to your royal position for such a time as this?

- Esther 4:14 NIV

When our heart hurts; God's heart also hurt with us.

He is for us, and He continues to fight on behalf of us, even when we don't see it.

In Esther's bravery, she saves her people. It shows that God does not abandon His people.

Be strong and courageous. Do not be afraid or terrified because of them, for the LORD your God goes with you; he will never leave you nor forsake you."

-Deuteronomy 31:6 NIV

Prayer:
Father, help me to trust you that you are bigger than any fear I have. Amen!

Think of This:
When fear causes hope to fade, there is God, the refuge you can reach on your knees.

Free Will

For you have been called to live in freedom, my brothers, and sisters. But don't use your freedom to satisfy your sinful nature. Instead, use your freedom to serve one another in love. - Galatians 5:13 NLT

Free will is granted to every man. If he desires to incline towards the good way and be righteous, he has the power to do it, and if he desires to incline towards the unrighteous way and be a wicked man, he has also the power to do so.

But!

This day I call the heavens and the earth as witnesses against you that I have set before you life and death, blessings, and curses. Now choose life, so that you and your children may live- Deuteronomy 30:19 NIV

We must serve one another in love.

Prayer:
Father God thank you for not looking your lowly people as king surveying his subject but as a tender loving Father; looking with joyful love at the children of His Kingdom.

Think of This:
Father's love is unfathomable.

Cycles of Blessings

Cast your bread upon the waters, for after many days you will find it again.
- Ecclesiastes 11:1 BSB

God's law of sowing and reaping is: "you work, you gain blessings" – salary.

If you give nothing, then nothing is what you get.

Generosity is our opportunity to serve our purpose, but this is not only in terms of money but service or work in the kingdom of God.

And do not be forgetful of the good, and of the sharing; for God is well pleased with such sacrifices. - Hebrews 13:16 BSB

Prayer:
Dear Father God thank you for blessing me that I can be a blessing to others.

Think of This:
God blesses us to bless others.

Left Over

When they had all had enough to eat, he said to his disciples, "Gather the pieces that are left over. Let nothing be wasted." -John 6:12 NIV

Jesus set us an example on thriftiness though He had an infinite supply at his disposal; He Himself is very economical, teaching us not to be wasteful.

Gather to save and which maybe useful to other persons or at another time. It's not His will that the things He made should go to waste without a cause. Just like us we can be a useful remnant.

For those whom He foreknew, He also predestined *to become* conformed to the image of His Son, - Romans 8:29 NASB

Prayer:
Father, your eye is on me as much as it is on the stars in the sky. Thank you for love and care and attention.

Think of This:
A remnant that is far from perfect but a remnant that trust God.

Compassion

Therefore, as God's chosen people, holy and dearly loved, clothe yourselves with compassion, kindness, humility, gentleness, and patience. – Colossians 3:12 NIV

When was the last time you wept for people?

Most of the time we love to talk but had a hard time listening. We want others to pay attention to every word we speak but have trouble paying attention to theirs.

Listen to someone's word and to their heart's cry. Those words, "I'm doing just fine!" But maybe their heart is crying out for help and compassion. The silent scream of the soul in anguish.

Rejoice with those who rejoice; mourn with those who mourn. - Romans 12:15 NIV

To love and to share God's word is one thing and to love those whom we shared God's word is quite another thing.

Prayer:

Father in heaven help us to celebrate together with those who rejoice and mourn with those who mourn and grow together in your healing love.

Think of This:

A big part of loving is listening.

Go and Share

"Return home and tell how much God has done for you." So, the man went away and told all over town how much Jesus had done for him." - Luke 8:39

God's transformational power in someone's life.

Our stories of pain and adversity are meant to serve as a testimony of God's faithfulness and power.

I've learned and understood that God designed us to go and share our story whether we want to or not because God doesn't want to waste our pain. Her has great plan and purpose and a beautiful future for all who believes in Him.

And we know that in all things God works for the good of those who love him, who have been called according to his purpose. -Romans 8:28 NIV

Prayer:
Father God thank you for all the pain and adversity that made me realize how much you love me and recognize your faithfulness and power over the matter. Amen!

Think of This:
The gospel is too good not to share.

The Plans of God

For I know the plans I have for you," declares the LORD, "plans to prosper you and not to harm you, plans to give you hope and a future. - Jeremiah 29:11 NIV

What is plan? Plan is an intention and decision about what one is going to do.

17 How precious to me are your thoughts, a God! How vast is the sum of them! Were I to count them, they would outnumber the grains of sand—when I awake, I am still with you. – Psalms 139:17-18 NIV

The thoughts and plans of God are like grains of sand; they are many. 2 Types of Plans

1. Man-made plans – Proverbs 16:1, Proverbs 19:21
2. God made plans – Jeremiah 29:11

Man made plans—every individual has his own unique projection and perception in life. Every day we make plans, especially in every major decision of our life.

God made plans—God has a plan for every one of us, but we at times take for granted the plans of God.

8"For my thoughts are not your thoughts, neither are your ways my ways," - Isaiah 55:8

Prayer:

Father we will not end as a loser because you are always here for us. Amen!

Think of This:

I assure you that if God puts plans and purpose in your life; you will never be dismayed.

Breaking-through Spiritual Barrenness

Look to Abraham, your father, and to Sarah, who gave you birth. When I called him, he was only one man, and I blessed him and made him many. – Isaiah 51:2

Barren means incapable of producing, unfruitful; it also means useless and futile.

2 Kinds of Barrenness

1. Physical Barrenness
2. Spiritual Barrenness

In History, traditionally in Israel, barren women are cursed. It resulted to rejection from society. Even in our times this is happening—physical barrenness.

While Spiritual barrenness is lack of growth—smallness, feeling of fear—intimidation, and poor self- concept—lack of vision.

Prayer:

Father, we pray that you keep us away from all forms of barrenness. Amen!

Think of This:

Examples of Barren Characters in the Bible:

1. Sarai or Sarah — Genesis 11:30
2. Hannah — 1 Samuel 1:5
3. Elizabeth – Luke 1:7
4. Rachel – Genesis 30:23

The Lord Calls

10The Lord came and stood there, calling as at the other times, "Samuel! Samuel!" Then Samuel said, "Speak, for your servant is listening." – 1 Samuel 3:10

Kindly Read 1 Samuel Chapter 3 verse 1 to 21.

Call means to say in a loud voice, demand, summon, request or petition.

Call is one of the common verbs in the Bible.

Call means to speak out in the way of prayer.

3'Call to me and I will answer you and tell you great and unsearchable things you do not know.' – Jeremiah 33:3

Prayer is called the telephone number of God. We call upon the name of the Lord and the assurance that God will answer us. But when you hear the phrase "The Lord Calls", What comes to your mind?

For so many people the Lord's call only refers to the lives of professional ministers. Examples: priest in Catholic religion, minister in Iglesia Ni Kristo. In Christian leadership there is a fivefold ministry: Apostles, prophets, evangelist, teachers, and pastors. But not only those minsters are called even you and I are called by God.

Prayer:
Father may we learn from the examples of those who are called in the Bible. Amen!

Think of This:
You have a calling.

The Lord Calls to Elijah

11The Lord said, "Go out and stand on the mountain in the presence of the Lord, for the Lord is about to pass by. Then a great and powerful wind tore the mountains apart and shattered the rocks before the Lord, but the Lord was not in the wind. After the wind there was an earthquake, but the Lord was not in the earthquake. 12After the earthquake came a fire, but the Lord was not in the fire. And after the fire came a gentle whisper. 13When Elijah heard it, he pulled his cloak over his face and went out and stood at the mouth of the cave. Then a voice said to him, "What are you doing here, Elijah? – 1 Kings 19:11-13

Elijah runaway for his life because of Jezebel. The Lord led Elijah to Mount Horeb where he waited for God to pass by. Then three powerful forces of nature came upon: (1) the wind, (2) the earthquake and (3) the fire.

The Lord was not in the wind. The Lord was not in the earthquake. The Lord was not on the fire. Elijah knew that God was not in these dramatic forces of nature but in a gentle whisper. A voice said to him, "What are you doing here Elijah?" He discovered the Lord's voice in a gentle breeze.

Are you listening for God? Or are you distracted by the dramatic forces of wind, earthquake, and fire?

The feeling of fear is a noise.

The Lord calls to Samuel four times.

Prayer:
 Father, we ask you to quiet the noises so that we can hear your life changing voice. Amen!

Think of This:
    Be sensitive like Elijah because God is calling you.

God Knew You

5"Before I formed you in the womb, I knew you, before you were born, I set you apart; I appointed you as a prophet to the nations." – Jeremiah 1:5

Look at the adverb: "I KNEW", it is in the past tense. When you are still a fetus in your mother's womb God already has a plan and purpose for you.

I want to share my life testimony:

I am a product of unwanted pregnancy. My mother wanted to abort me, intentionally to kill me. but because has a plan for me, I live and I'm alive.

Why God has a plan?

I believe in the story of creation everything is provided for us to live. A kind of life like a paradise. Wow! It's beautiful. According to Psalms 8:4, God is mindful of us. He is an all-knowing God. So whatever agonies and anxieties; whatever pain you have right now, remember that God is mindful about you.

Prayer:
Father give us faith as we entrust you all the pain and sufferings we have right now. Amen!

Think of This:
When you cry, nothing is hidden, God knows it. He is mindful of you. He is so concern of you.

You Will Bear Much Fruit

5"I am the vine; you are the branches. If you remain in me and I in you, you will bear much fruit; apart from me you can do nothing. - John 15:5

How to get out of barrenness?

1. For one to get out of barrenness; one must be blessed by God. A.

    Jesus wants to start with little.

    > When I called him, he was only one man, and I blessed him and made him many. -Isaiah 51:2

    > 6"Alas, Sovereign Lord," I said, "I do not know how to speak; I am too young.7But the Lord said to me, "Do not say, 'I am too young.' You must go to everyone I send you to and say whatever I command you. 8Do not be afraid of them, for I am with you and will rescue you," declares the Lord.9Then the Lord reached out his hand and touched my mouth and said to me, "I have put my words in your mouth. 10See, today I appoint you over nations and kingdoms to uproot and tear down, to destroy and overthrow, to build and to plant. "Jeremiah 1:610

    God used Jeremiah even though he was a child. B.

    But to remain little is not of God.

2. For one to get out of barrenness he or she shall multiply in Him.

Prayer:

> Father, we ask that you make our life fruitful. Amen!

Think of This:

> God is going to deliver you from the curse of barrenness through divine intervention.

You Are Blessed

2Dear friend, I pray that you may enjoy good health and that all may go well with you, even as your soul is getting along well. - 3 John 1:2

God wants to bless us in all areas of life. Prosperity is an abundant supply. God can make all grace abounds.

We have a living hope in Christ. Let's persevere in hope as we wait patiently for his deliverance.

Praise be to the God and Father of our Lord Jesus Christ! In his great mercy he has given us new birth into a living hope through the resurrection of Jesus Christ from the dead. 1 Peter 1:3

There is surely a future hope for you. As the song "Because He lives" says,

"I Know he holds the future." What are the plans of God?

1. To prosper you and not harm you
2. To give you hope
3. To give you a future

Prayer:
Father God thank you that you have designed me to be blessed. Amen!

Think of This:
Have you considered God to your plans for your life? Is the will of the Father important to you?
God's will and plan is the Best!

Is There Anything Too Hard For The Lord?

Is anything too hard for the LORD? I will return to you at the appointed time next year, and Sarah will have a son."- Genesis 18:14

That is Divine Intervention—only God can!

Multiplication is a dream of God.

The LORD took him outside and said, "Look at the sky and try to count the stars; you will have as many descendants as that."– Genesis 15:5

So those who have faith are blessed along with Abraham the man of faith. -Galatians 3:9

And on the morrow, when they were come from Bethany, he was hungry: And seeing a fig tree afar off having leaves, he came, if haply he might find any thing thereon: and when he came to it, he found nothing but leaves; for the time of figs was not *yet*. And Jesus answered and said unto it, No man eat fruit of thee hereafter forever. And his disciples heard *it*. – Mark 11:12-14

Jesus cursed the fig tree because of its unfruitfulness.

We need to multiply! How?

Go ye therefore, and teach all nations, baptizing them in the name of the Father, and of the Son, and of the Holy Ghost: -Matthew 28:19

All disciples of Jesus Christ are believers but not all believers are disciples.

Prayer:
Father God, we pray that you break the spirit of barrenness and pour out the spirit of fruitfulness. Amen!

Think of This:
We are called to make disciples. We are called to be fruitful and multiply and not to be barren.

Voice of God

When God speaks that is the audible voice of God in the Old Testament. And Samuel told Elli about the message of God.

In New Testament, part of listening is expecting God to speak from His Spirit to ours. Though not audible his communication can see even louder than a voice.

But God hath revealed them unto us by his Spirit: for the Spirit searcheth all things, yea, the deep things of God. – 1 Corinthians 2:10

Remember to do what He says and write it down. Most of us forget if we don't write. The mind is for thinking and the pen is for remembering. Keep our focus on the Lord is also important.

We have the responsibility to answer the call by obediently following Him. no matter the consequence believe that you can do whatever he is called you to do.

I can do all things through Christ which strengtheneth me. – Philipians 4:13

And the Lord calls you to service.
For we are his workmanship, created in Christ Jesus unto good works, which God hath before ordained that we should walk in them. – Ephesians 2:10

Make His call in your life clear. You are called to serve.

Find yourself fruitful and effective if you know you are called.

Prayer:
        Father God may we always hear and listen to your still small voice. Amen!

Think of This:
        This means each of us has very specific and important assignment or job to do in the Kingdom of God.

Breaking-through Spiritual Barrenness

What little you have?

Let us Give to Lord Because the little becomes much when it is place in the Master's hand.

And they had a few small fishes: and he blessed and commanded to set. them also before them. 8So they did eat and were filled: and they took up of the broken meat that was left seven baskets. – Mark 8:7-8

Give our talent to God.

And unto one he gave five talents, to another two, and to another one. to every man according to his several abilities; and straightway took his journey. – Matthew 25:15

I am the vine, ye are the branches: He that abideth in me, and I in him, the same bringeth forth much fruit: for without me ye can do nothing. – John 15:5

Prayer:

Father God, we renounce barrenness in our life. In the name of Jesus Christ. Amen!

Think of This:

Desire now breakthrough! And let us begin to multiply, let us begin to increase and become fruitful for this is the will of God.

About the Authors:

Ariane A. Villena

Currently residing in Makati City and working as part-time Graphic Artist of Kingdomson Trading and a full-time mother to her two daughters. She is a certified coach of IKMA Philippines and one of the teachers of IKMA Discipleship since 2022. You can also watch her in IKMA Muntinlupa Facebook Page, as she hosts the online program, "Mana Sa Ama."

Belina G. Laquindanum

Born on Feb. 19, 1960. Married to Claudio David Laquindanum Sr. and Senior Pastor of Mighty Presence Kingdom Church Inc. Located at #250 purok 3, Nueva Victoria, Mexico, Pampanga. She has 4 children: Jomar, Stephen Carl, Shiela Ann, and Claudio Jr. and 5 grandchildren: Steven Luke, Amos Jabez, Caleb Josiah, Carl Isaiah, and David Jase. **Arnna Williams Frazier** Kingdom Daughter, Mother, Student and Community Caregiver.

Ruby Villar

Born in Philippines and graduated with Bachelor of Science Degree in Business Management and received credit hours on Education and worked as a preschool teacher. She has also worked as Duty Manager in the biggest drug store in Cavite, Philippines. She is passionate on teaching children especially about Bible stories and how to love as a kingdom mandate. **Nenita D. Dulce** Born in Gen. Trias Cavite, Philippines, a mother of 2 sons and currently works for 12 years as Pharmacy Asst. Though she is silent and shy, she is active in helping with elders, music, worship team and bible studies ministries in Christ to All Nations Church. She is appreciative of the knowledge gained through the mentorship program about identity as she quoted "Now our identity produces our destiny."- Nancy Bocalan.

Notes:

Notes:

Notes:

Made in the USA
Middletown, DE
17 July 2023

34708820R00038